GW01396055

FASCINATING BiBLE FACTS

VOL. 2

FASCINATING BIBLE FACTS

VOL. 2

104 DEVOTIONS

IRENE HOWAT

Published by
Christian Focus Publications,
Geanies House, Fearn, Tain, Ross-shire,
IV20 1TW, Scotland, U.K.

www.christianfocus.com
email: info@christianfocus.com

Cover design by Thomas Barnard
Illustrations by Tim Charnick
Printed and bound in Europe

For my friend Sharon,
with thanks.

Contents

GET STARTED

Here are 104 facts for you to discover about God and his Word – the Bible.

Look out for the Fact Finders: Chloe, Zac and Abbi. Chloe has questions, Zac is ready with a challenge or two and Abbi has some useful information to add to all the facts.

After each fact there is a promise from God. These promises are repeated in slightly different words and in different places in the Bible.

Look out for Chloe, Zac and Abbi throughout the book.

Chloe

Zac

Abbi

WHAT IS A FACT?

A fact is something that is certain, sure and true, something so reliable that we can use it as the basis of our lives. The Bible is true because it is the Word of God and God cannot tell lies. Therefore all the stories quoted in this book are factual and true.

Fascinating Bible Facts Vol. 2 also includes many promises of God. But how can promises be facts? They can when God makes them! When we make a promise we try to keep it, but the Lord is so wonderful that all his promises are as good as kept the moment he makes them. So the promises of God are facts – certain, sure and true – and we can safely base our lives on them. God the Lord will never, ever, ever let us down.

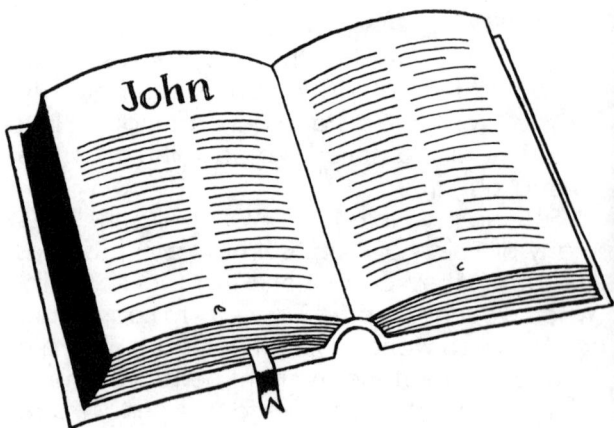

KNOWING NAMES

1 Where does the name Bible come from? It has a long history, going back to the days when people wrote on parchment. The Egyptian word for parchment was 'byblos'. The Greeks used that word to mean a scroll, and they changed it to 'biblion'. Their word for a collection of books, a library, was 'biblia'. That's where we get the word Bible.

So now you know some ancient Egyptian and Greek!

BIBLE PROMISE: 'If any of you lacks wisdom, he should ask God, who gives generously to all without finding fault; and it will be given to him' (James 1:5).

2 The name Jesus also has a meaning. In fact, most Bible names have meanings. Many names still have meanings today. Susan means lily and it comes from ancient Hebrew. Peter comes from the Greek word for stone.

Read Matthew 1:21 to discover what the name Jesus means, and it must be right, for it's an angel who is speaking! The angel told Joseph, Mary 'will give birth to a son, and you are to give him the name Jesus, because he will save his people from their sins.' The name Jesus means SAVIOUR.

Jesus means Saviour.

BIBLE PROMISE: 'Whether you turn to the right or to the left, your ears will hear a voice behind you saying, "This is the way; walk in it"' (Isaiah 30:21).

3 Much of the book of Genesis tells the story of Abraham, but that wasn't his name to start with. The name his parents chose for their baby son was Abram, which means 'exalted father.' Isn't that a strange name to call your baby son! Presumably they hoped that one day he would be a father and that his family would think highly of him.

God changed Abram's name to Abraham (Genesis 17:5), which means 'Father of many'. That was an especially good name as the Lord had just told him that he would become the father of many nations!

• •

ZAC'S CHALLENGE: Write out the books of the Old and New Testaments and see if you can memorise them!

BIBLE PROMISE: 'Surely goodness and love will follow me all the days of my life, and I will dwell in the house of the LORD for ever' (Psalm 23:6).

4 Abraham and his wife Sarah were still childless and much too old to have children, but he still believed God's promise that he would become the father of many nations.

When the Lord told Abraham, who was nearly 100, that they would have a son in a year's time, Sarah overheard what was said and laughed. God's promise came true and one year later their little son was born. They called him Issac, which means 'He Laughs' in the Hebrew language. (Genesis 21:3-6)

●●●●●●●●●●●●●●●●●●●●●●●●●●●●●●●●●●●●●●●

ABBI'S INFO: Isaac and Rebekah had twin sons, Esau and Jacob. Esau means red or hairy and he was both red and hairy. Jacob means 'The Deceiver'. The name suited Jacob. He was a deceiver until the Lord changed his heart. (Genesis 25:25-26)

BIBLE PROMISE: 'But he (Jesus) was pierced for our transgressions, he was crushed for our iniquities; the punishment that brought us peace was upon him, and by his wounds we are healed' (Isaiah 53:5).

5 Esau and Jacob were forever fighting. Eventually Jacob had to run away to escape from his brother. However, he could not run away from God.

Once Jacob had a dream in which he saw a ladder going from earth to heaven, with angels climbing up and down it. From the top of the ladder God spoke to Jacob, telling him that he and his descendants would be blessed. Jacob named the place where he had his dream Bethel, which means 'House of God'. (Genesis 28:19)

BIBLE PROMISE: 'When we were overwhelmed by sins, you forgave our transgressions' (Psalm 65:3).

6 Some years later, when Jacob and his family were going to see Esau, he had a strange experience. In a way that we don't understand he spent a night wrestling with the Lord. Afterwards God changed Jacob's name to Israel, which means 'He struggles with God'. (Genesis 32:28)

The place where that happened changed its name too. It became Peniel, which means 'face of God', because at that place he had seen the face of God and lived. (Genesis 32:30).

Jacob's descendants were called 'The children of Israel' or 'Israelites'. (Exodus 1:7) Even today they bear his name, though changed a little bit, for they are known as 'Israelis'.

• •

CHLOE'S QUESTIONS: What is the ancient Greek word for library?

BIBLE PROMISE: 'The sun will no more be your light by day, nor will the brightness of the moon shine on you, for the LORD will be your everlasting light, and your God will be your glory' (Isaiah 60:19).

7 The second book of the Bible, Exodus, gets its name from an amazing event that's described in the book.

After the children of Israel had been slaves in Egypt for a long time, God raised up Moses to lead them out of captivity. Remember the story? Pharaoh's heart was hard and he wouldn't let God's people go, even though the Lord sent nine plagues on the country. Only after the tenth and most awful plague did Pharaoh allow Moses to lead the children of Israel out of Egypt and towards God's Promised Land.

So what does the word Exodus mean? It means 'a mass departure of people'. The book of Exodus is well named as about 600,000 men, as well as women and children, departed from Egypt that day. It certainly was a mass departure! (Exodus chapters 6 to 12).

● ●

CHLOE'S QUESTIONS: What is the ancient Greek word for a scroll?

BIBLE PROMISE: 'Though outwardly we are wasting away, yet inwardly we are bring renewed day by day' (2 Corinthians 4:16).

8 When Moses was working as a shepherd, he saw a bush burning that was not burnt out. From the burning bush the Lord spoke to him, telling Moses that he was specially chosen to save the children of Israel from the Egyptians.

Moses knew that nobody would pay any attention to him, and he asked God what his name was in order that he could tell the people who had sent him. God told Moses his name. His name is 'I am who I am'. Moses had to tell the Israelites that 'I AM' had sent him (Exodus 3:14).

• •

BIBLE PROMISE: God says, 'I will heal their waywardness and love them freely, for my anger has turned away from them' (Hosea 14:4).

9 After Pharaoh released the Israelites from slavery they wandered for forty years before reaching God's Promised Land. During that time they grumbled a lot about their food.

God sent them manna from heaven. It lay like frost on the ground for them to collect and eat. Manna means 'What is it?' Can you imagine the first time they saw it? They would have asked each other, 'What is it?' And the name stuck! (Exodus 16:31)

ABBI'S INFO: To find out about Moses' early life read Exodus chapters 2 and 3. His sister's name was Miriam and his mother's name was Jochabed.

BIBLE PROMISE: 'But God will redeem my life from the grave; he will surely take me to himself' (Psalm 49:15).

10 The fifth book of the Bible is called Deuteronomy, which comes from two Greek words 'deuteros', meaning second, and 'nomos', meaning law. It contains the Ten Commandments. Deuteronomy also contains many other laws given by God to help his people live their lives well.

Joshua (the sixth book of the Bible is called after him) succeeded Moses as the leader of the Israelites, and when he died there was nobody to take over from him. Instead of having one leader, God gave his people a series of fifteen judges, whose job was to keep the Israelites living how the Lord wanted them to live. The people failed God often, but he never once failed them. The story of the fifteen judges is told in the book named … Judges. It's obvious, isn't it?

• •

CHLOE'S QUESTIONS: What does the word 'manna' mean?

BIBLE PROMISE: The LORD says, 'Fear not, for I have redeemed you; I have summoned you by name; you are mine' (Isaiah 43:1).

The LORD watches over all who love him. (Psalm 145:20)

WHO'S WHO?

11 Many Bible books are named after the person who wrote them, or the person about whom the books are written.
The book of Ruth is a love story with a twist, because Ruth and her husband Boaz have a little baby boy who turned out to be the grandfather of King David! The Book of Ruth is just four chapters long. It's a really good short story.

. . . .

ABBI'S INFO: Ruth's baby boy turned out to be the great, great, (and many other greats!) grandfather of the Lord Jesus Christ!

BIBLE PROMISE: 'But if we walk in the light, as he is in the light, we have fellowship with one another, and the blood of Jesus, his Son, purifies us from all sin' (1 John 1:7).

12

Because the Israelite people had disobeyed God so often the Lord exiled them to Babylon and allowed Jerusalem to be destroyed, temple and all.

The book of Nehemiah is named after ... Nehemiah. No surprises there! Nehemiah worked in the King of Babylon's palace but he was given time off to organise the rebuilding of the walls of Jerusalem. Three wicked men tried to put him off the work, inviting him to a place called Ono to discuss things. Nehemiah knew better. When asked to go to Ono, he said, 'Oh no!' (Nehemiah 6:1-4)

• •

CHLOE'S QUESTIONS: Which is the fifth book in the Bible? What does the word 'Exodus' mean?

BIBLE PROMISE: 'The LORD watches over all who love him, but all the wicked he will destroy' (Psalm 145:20).

24

13 The Book of Esther is named after an Israelite woman who became Queen of Babylon. She was used by the Lord to save her people from extermination. Interestingly, the words 'God' and 'Lord' don't appear in the Book of Esther at all even though she was a woman of great faith and courage. (Esther 2:12-16)

BIBLE PROMISE: 'For if you forgive men when they sin against you, your heavenly Father will also forgive you' (Matthew 6:14).

14 The book of Lamentations was written by Jeremiah and was given its name because he was lamenting (that means mourning) the destruction of the first temple in Jerusalem. Yet right in the middle of the book Jeremiah says some really encouraging words.

'Because of the LORD's great love we are not consumed, for his compassions never fail. They are new every morning; great is your faithfulness' (Lamentations 3:22-23).

These wonderful words remind us that even when life is really difficult, God cares for his people.

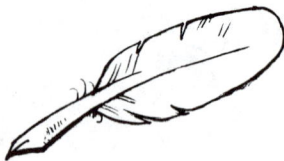

BIBLE PROMISE: 'For just as the Father raises the dead and gives them life, even so the Son gives life to whom he is pleased to give it' (John 5:21).

15

The first four books of the New Testament are the names of the four men who wrote them.

Matthew, who was a tax collector, followed Jesus and became a disciple (Matthew 9:9).

Mark was the son of Mary, in whose home it's thought that the Last Supper was held (Acts 12:12).

Luke was a doctor who joined Paul in his missionary work (Colossians 4:14).

John and his brother James were among Jesus' first followers (Mark 1:19-20).

The Book of Acts is actually called The Acts of the Apostles, and it tells the story of the early church. It was written by Dr Luke and is part two of his gospel story.

BIBLE PROMISE: 'He will teach us his ways, so that we may walk in his paths' (Micah 4:2).

16 The final book of the New Testament, and of the whole Bible, is Revelation. A revelation is something that's made known, and in this wonderful book God made known to John in a vision some amazing facts about heaven. Here is one of them: John saw that '… God himself will be with them and be their God. He will wipe every tear from their eyes. There will be no more death or mourning or crying or pain …' (Revelation 21:3-4).

Much of John's vision is too amazing for our human minds to take in, but from it we know that heaven will be wonderful beyond anything we can think or imagine.

BIBLE PROMISE: In him (Jesus), we have redemption through his blood, the forgiveness of sins, in accordance with the riches of God's grace that he lavished on us with all wisdom and understanding' (Ephesians 1:7).

'Through Jesus the forgiveness of sins is proclaimed to you'

(Acts 13:38)

THE BIRTH OF JESUS

17 Throughout Old Testament times God told his people about the Saviour who was to come. Over hundreds of years a picture built up. Then, when Jesus was born, those who knew God's prophesies saw things falling into place. Here is one being fulfilled 800 years after it was made!

Prophecy - 'But you, Bethlehem Ephrathah, though you are small among the clans of Judah, out of you will come for me one who will be ruler over Israel' (Micah 5:2).

Fulfilment – 'The shepherds said to one another, "Let's go to Bethlehem and see this thing that has happened, which the Lord has told us about. So they hurried off and found Mary and Joseph, and the baby, who was lying in the manger' (Luke 2:15-16).

. . . .

BIBLE PROMISE: '... if anyone does sin, we have one who speaks to the Father in our defence – Jesus Christ, the Righteous One' (1 John 2:1).

18

Prophecy – 'Therefore the Lord himself will give you a sign: The virgin will be with child and will give birth to a son, and will call him Immanuel' (Isaiah 7:14).

Fulfilment – 'In the sixth month, God sent the angel Gabriel to Nazareth, a town in Galilee, to a virgin …' 'The angel said to her, "Do not be afraid, Mary, you have found favour with God. You will be with child and give birth to a son, and you are to give him the name Jesus."' (Luke 1:26, 30-31)

Immanuel means 'God with us' and, when Jesus was born, God was with the human race in a very special way.

BIBLE PROMISE: 'Come, let us bow down in worship, let us kneel before the Lᴏʀᴅ our Maker, for he is our God and we are the people of his pasture, the flock under his care' (Psalm 95:6).

19 **Prophecy** – 'The kings of Tarshish and of distant shores will bring tribute to him; the kings of Sheba and Seba will present him gifts' (Psalm 72:10).

Fulfilment – 'After Jesus was born in Bethlehem in Judea, during the time of King Herod, Magi from the east came to Jerusalem and asked, "Where is the one who has been born king of the Jews? We saw his star in the east and have come to worship him …"

'On coming to the house, they saw the child with his mother Mary, and they bowed down and worshipped him. Then they opened their treasures and presented him with gifts of gold and of incense and of myrrh' (Matthew 2:1-2, 11).

BIBLE PROMISE: 'I write to you, dear children, because your sins have been forgiven on account of his (Jesus') name' (1 John 2:12).

20

Prophecy – '"When Israel was a child, I loved him, and out of Egypt I called my son"' (Hosea 11:1).

Fulfilment – 'When they (the Magi) had gone, an angel of the Lord appeared to Joseph in a dream. "Get up," he said, "take the child and his mother and escape to Egypt. Stay there until I tell you, for Herod is going to search for the child to kill him." So he got up, took the child and his mother during the night and left for Egypt. ... After Herod died, an angel of the Lord appeared in a dream to Joseph in Egypt and said, "Get up, take the child and his mother and go to the land of Israel, for those who were trying to take the child's life are dead"' (Matthew :13-15, 19-20).

BIBLE PROMISE: 'The LORD is gracious and compassionate, slow to anger and rich in love' (Psalm 145:8).

21

Prophecy – 'This is what the Lord says: "A voice is heard in Ramah, mourning and great weeping, Rachel weeping for her children and refusing to be comforted, because her children are no more"' (Jeremiah 31:15).

Fulfilment – 'When Herod realised that he had been outwitted by the Magi, he was furious, and he gave orders to kill all the boys in Bethlehem and its vicinity who were two years old and under, in accordance with the time he had learned from the Magi' (Matthew 2:16).

No wonder the poor women were weeping.

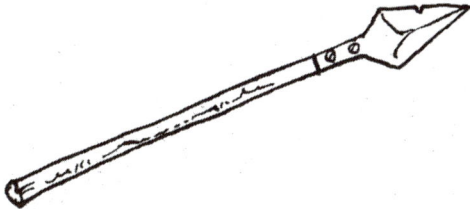

BIBLE PROMISE: 'Because of the Lord's great love we are not consumed, for his compassions never fail' (Lamentations 3:22).

'And after my skin has been destroyed, yet in my flesh I will see God'.

(Job 19:26)

THE NAMES OF JESUS

22 When we are babies our parents often use pet names for us. When we fall in love we might find ourselves called 'Sweetheart' or 'Darling', and perhaps one day 'Dad' or 'Mum'. The Lord Jesus has many names.

Remember Job and all his troubles? Right in the midst of his terrible situation, he made a wonderful statement about Jesus, who would not be born till hundreds of years afterwards. Job said, 'I know that my Redeemer lives ... I myself will see him with my own eyes – I, and not another. How my heart yearns within me!' (Job 19:25-27). God showed him that the Redeemer would come, and that Redeemer was Jesus.

A redeemer is someone who buys something. The Lord showed Job that his soul would be bought by Jesus and that one day he would see his Redeemer face to face.

● ●

BIBLE PROMISE: 'With God we shall gain the victory, and he will trample down our enemies' (Psalm 60:12).

23 It was about 800 years before Jesus was born that Isaiah spoke about the Saviour's birth. He said he would be called Immanuel, which means 'God with us'.

When Jesus was born on earth that's just what he was, God in human flesh living among ordinary human beings! (Isaiah 7:14)

BIBLE PROMISE: God says, 'Their sins and lawless acts I will remember no more' (Hebrews 10:17).

24 Strangely Isaiah then called Jesus 'Everlasting Father'. How can Jesus be God the Father as well as being God's Son?

Isaiah had no way of really understanding it, but this is one of the Old Testament clues that help us to understand that, while God is one God, he is three persons – the Father, the Son and the Holy Spirit. (Isaiah 9:6)

The word we use for God in three persons is the Trinity.

• •

BIBLE PROMISE: 'All mankind will fear; they will proclaim the works of God and ponder what he has done' (Psalm 64:9).

25 Another Old Testament prophet, Zechariah, called Jesus a fountain that would cleanse his people from sin and impurity. What does a fountain do? The water in a fountain can be used for washing. (Zechariah 13:1)

When we come to the Lord Jesus in faith he washes us from all our dirty sins. Absolutely all our sins look filthy to God, even the very smallest white lie.

● ●

BIBLE PROMISE: '... through faith (we) are shielded by God's power until the coming of the salvation that is ready to be revealed in the last time' (1 Peter 1:5).

26

What a surprise it must have been to Mary to be told by an angel that she was to have a baby and that her baby would be called 'the Son of God'! But that's exactly what happened. Jesus had no human father. God gave Joseph the special job of bringing up Jesus as though he were his son. (Luke 1:35)

God's angel told Joseph that Mary was to give birth to the Son of God, and that his name was to be Jesus.

When Jesus was baptised, God's voice confirmed Jesus' identity when he spoke from heaven calling him 'my Son, whom I love.'

What a wonderful name for Jesus, God's beloved Son. (Matthew 3:17)

CHLOE'S QUESTIONS: How did Zechariah describe Jesus?

BIBLE PROMISE: John the Baptist recognised who Jesus is and what he had come to do when he said, 'Look, the Lamb of God, who takes away the sin of the world!' (John 1:29).

27

When John began his gospel he didn't start with the birth of Jesus. He opened the story of the life of Jesus with the words, 'In the beginning was the Word, and the Word was with God, and the Word was God.'

Remember, right back at the beginning of the Bible God created by his Word. Who was that Word? He was Jesus. He was right in there at creation all those years before he was born at Bethlehem. (John 1:1)

BIBLE PROMISE: 'My son, do not despise the Lord's discipline and do not resent his rebuke, because the Lord disciplines those he loves, as a father the son he delights in' (Proverbs 3:11-12).

28

In John 1:41, Andrew tells his brother Peter, '"We have found the Messiah" (that is the Christ).' The Jews knew that God had promised that a Saviour would come and they referred to him as the Messiah, which means 'God's anointed one'. The name Christ means just the same thing in Greek.

One day two blind men called out to Jesus to help them. Amazingly, they shouted, 'Have mercy on us, Son of David.' They knew God had promised that a special son from the family of King David would come to save his people. They recognised Jesus was that one. Isn't it interesting that two blind men could see in their hearts and minds what sighted people could not see? (Matthew 9:27)

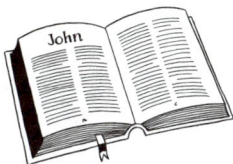

BIBLE PROMISE: God 'will judge the world in righteousness and the peoples in his truth' (Psalm 96:13).

29

Jesus gave himself some names. One of them was 'the Good Shepherd'.

The job of the shepherd in Jesus' day was to care for the sheep regardless of his own health and safety. Jesus went on to say, 'The good shepherd lays down his life for his sheep.' That's exactly what he did. (John 10:11)

Nobody took the Lord's life from him, he laid down his own life in order to take the punishment for our sins so that we could go free and go to heaven. What a Good Shepherd we have!

BIBLE PROMISE: 'Taste and see that the Lord is good; blessed is the man who takes refuge in him' (Psalm 34:8).

30 Another of Jesus' unusual names for himself is 'the true vine' and he says that those who believe in him are the branches! Are you a branch in Jesus? What does he mean by that?

The Lord is telling us that, if we want to be fruitful in our lives, we need to be attached to him. We are attached to Jesus when we trust him as our Saviour.

Not only does Jesus say that he is the true vine and we are the branches, he tells us that his father is the gardener! So God the Father is like a gardener looking after all those who are attached to Jesus. (John 15:1-4)

If you read Galatians 5:22-23 you'll discover the kind of fruit that our heavenly Gardener will produce in our lives.

●●●●●●●●●●●●●●●●●●●●●●●●●●●●●●●●

BIBLE PROMISE: Jesus says, 'Blessed are the pure in heart, for they will see God' (Matthew 5:8).

31

The Apostle Paul wrote of Jesus being 'the Rock'.

Houses built on rocks never sink into the ground and houses built on sand are washed away in the first flood, according to a story Jesus told.

Lives built on the rock that is Jesus are safe for all eternity. Lives built on any other foundation will eventually come to grief. (1 Corinthians 10:4).

You can read this dramatic short story for yourself in Matthew 7:24-27.

BIBLE PROMISE: Jesus says, 'Whoever believes in the Son has eternal life, but whoever rejects the Son will not see life, for God's wrath remains on him' (John 3:36).

3 2

The last book of the Bible is a vision John was given of heaven. In it Jesus gives us a strange name for himself. He says he is 'the Alpha and the Omega'. (Revelation 1:8)

If you knew Greek, it would not be so strange. Alpha and omega are the first and the last letters of the Greek alphabet, just like our A and Z.

Jesus is using this name for himself to show that he is eternal, that he was there before the beginning of things and that he will be there forever.

There are many other names in the Bible for Jesus. You'll find some of them in Matthew 2:23, 8:20, John 8:12, 10:7, 14:6 and Hebrews 12:2.

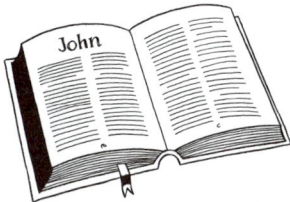

BIBLE PROMISE: 'Then you will call, and the LORD will answer; you will cry for help, and he will say: "Here am I"' (Isaiah 58:9).

Repent, for the kingdom of heaven is near'.
(Matthew 4:17)

FACTS ABOUT JESUS

33 In the Old Testament the Lord told Isaiah about John the Baptist coming before Jesus. He was to be, 'A voice of one calling: "In the desert prepare the way for the Lord, make straight in the wilderness a highway for our God' (Isaiah 40:3).

Jesus coming to earth was so amazing and so wonderful that God sent John the Baptist to prepare the way for him and to prepare people to hear what Jesus had to say.

• •

BIBLE PROMISE: Of those who fear the LORD – '"They will be mine," says the LORD Almighty, "in the day when I make up my treasured possession. I will spare them, just as in compassion a man spares his son who serves him'" (Malachi 3:17).

34

Hundreds of years before Jesus was born God said that he would teach by using parables (stories with a meaning). Here it is in Psalm 78:1-3. 'O my people, hear my teaching; listen to the words of my mouth. I will open my mouth in parables ...'

In Matthew 13:34-35 the prophecy is fulfilled. 'Jesus spoke all these things to the crowd in parables; he did not say anything to them without using a parable.'

Matthew, who knew his Bible (our Old Testament) went on to say, 'So was fulfilled what was spoken through the prophet: "I will open my mouth in parables, I will utter things hidden since the creation of the world."'

• •

CHLOE'S QUESTIONS: What are the first and last letters of the Greek alphabet?

BIBLE PROMISE: Jesus says, 'In my Father's house are many rooms; if it were not so, I would have told you. I am going there to prepare a place for you. And if I go and prepare a place for you, I will come back and take you to be with me that you also may be where I am' (John 14:2-3).

35

There's a wonderful prophecy about Jesus in Isaiah. 'Then will the eyes of the blind be opened and the ears of the deaf unstopped. Then will the lame leap like a deer, and the tongue of the dumb shout for joy ...' (Isaiah 35:5-6).

Every part of that is fulfilled in the life of Jesus! The eyes of several blind people were opened and they were able to see. You'll find the story of a blind beggar in Luke 18:35-43.

BIBLE PROMISE: 'He who is the Glory of Israel does not lie or change his mind; for he is not a man, that he should change his mind' (1 Samuel 15:29).

36

Because Jesus performed miracles, news about him spread around the whole area. Sometimes that even caused problems. Mark tells us that so many people came to Jesus, that he was not able to speak!

'That evening after sunset the people brought to Jesus all the sick and demon-possessed. The whole town gathered at the door, and Jesus healed many who had various diseases. He also drove out many demons, but he would not let the demons speak because they knew who he was' (Mark 1:32-34).

● ●

CHLOE'S QUESTIONS: What does the word 'parable' mean?

BIBLE PROMISE: 'The LORD is near to all who call on him, to all who call on him in truth' (Psalm 145:18).

37

The prophet Zechariah was told by God how the Lord Jesus would arrive in Jerusalem. 'See, your king comes to you, righteous and having salvation, gentle and riding on a donkey, on a colt, the foal of a donkey' (Zechariah 9:9).

Generations later that's exactly what happened. The disciples, 'brought the donkey and the colt, placed their cloaks on them, and Jesus sat on them' (Matthew 21:7).

BIBLE PROMISE: 'Let the wicked forsake his way and the evil man his thoughts. Let him turn to the Lord, and he will have mercy on him, and to our God, for he will freely pardon' (Isaiah 55:7).

38

Jesus' death for sinners was foretold to Isaiah. '... he was cut off from the land of the living; for the transgression of my people he was stricken' (Isaiah 53:8). And the New Testament tells us that is true. 'While we were still sinners, Christ died for us' (Romans 5:8).

It is no surprise that God's prophecies come to pass. God is Truth and he cannot tell lies.

BIBLE PROMISE: 'Though the mountains be shaken and the hills be removed, yet my unfailing love for you will not be shaken nor my covenant of peace be removed,' says the LORD, who has compassion on you (Isaiah 54:10).

39

Jesus was a Jew, and he came to bring the good news about the forgiveness of sins to his own people and also to Gentiles (Gentiles are those who are not Jewish).

God told that to Isaiah nearly 800 years earlier. 'I will also make you a light for the Gentiles, that you may bring my salvation to the ends of the earth' (Isaiah 49:6).

When the news about Jesus began to spread, Paul and Barnabas told the Jews, 'We had to speak the word of God to you first. Since you reject it and do not consider yourselves worthy of eternal life, we now turn to the Gentiles. For this is what the Lord has commanded us: "I have made you a light for the Gentiles, that you may bring salvation to the ends of the earth"' (Acts 13:46-47).

BIBLE PROMISE: God's angelic messenger told Joseph – 'She (Mary) will give birth to a son, and you are to give him the name Jesus, because he will save his people from their sins' (Matthew 1:21).

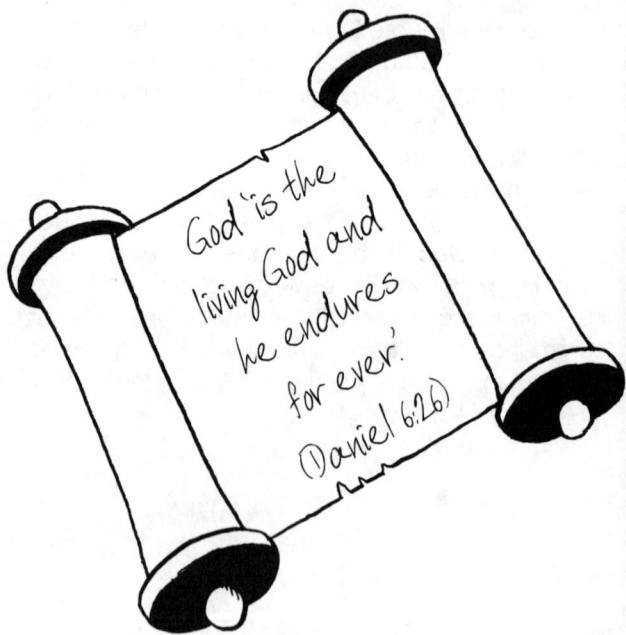

God `is the
living God and
he endures
for ever.'
(Daniel 6:26)

MAGNIFICENT MIRACLES !

40 What is a miracle? A miracle is something quite outside of what happens naturally. It is truly supernatural. There are miracles in the Bible apart from those done by Jesus, but we'll stick to the ones he did.

We should not be surprised that Jesus did miracles. Why should the one who made the laws of nature not change or suspend them if he chooses?

The biggest miracle of all, and it truly is a miracle, is that the Lord Jesus Christ, the king of Kings and lord of Lords, should come down from his throne of glory and humble himself, becoming a little baby in order to die to save us from our sins. We just can't take that in! (Philippians 2:6-8)

• •

BIBLE PROMISE: 'Therefore, there is now no condemnation for those who are in Christ Jesus' (Romans 8:1).

41 One day a man suffering from leprosy came to Jesus and knelt before him. 'Lord, if you are willing, you can make me clean.' That poor man was absolutely right in what he said. Jesus is able to do anything he is willing to do.

Before he healed the man, Jesus reached out and touched him. Lepers were 'untouchables' but Jesus touched him. The Lord's touch must have been like a bolt of lightning through the man. Then Jesus said, 'I am willing. Be clean.' And he was! (Matthew 8:1-4)

● ●

BIBLE PROMISE: 'You have made known to me the path of life; you will fill me with joy in your presence, with eternal pleasures at your right hand' (Psalm 16:11).

42 Imagine being invited out for a meal and then arriving to find your hostess in bed with a high temperature. I guess most of us would just go home. Jesus didn't. He healed his hostess who then got up and served the meal! (Matthew 8:14-15)

Jesus was not a doctor who healed people, he is God who commanded diseases and evil spirits to come out of the people they were troubling. (Matthew 4:16)

BIBLE PROMISE: God 'is the living God and he endures for ever; his kingdom will not be destroyed, his dominion will never end' (Daniel 6:26).

59

43 When four men brought their paralysed friend to Jesus they probably expected the Lord to tell him to get up and walk. Instead he told the man that his sins were forgiven. No wonder the teachers of the law were furious for only God could do that!

Jesus chose his words carefully because he was telling them that he was indeed God. Then he told the man to get up, roll up his mat and go home. (Matthew 9:1-8)

How grateful that man must have been – forgiven and healed at the same time!

● ●

BIBLE PROMISE: Jesus said, 'I tell you, whoever acknowledges me before men, the Son of Man will also acknowledge him before the angels of God' (Luke 12:8).

44 Jesus was on his way to heal a dying twelve-year-old girl, when a woman who had been ill for twelve years came to him for healing. Jesus spent so long talking to the woman that the little girl died. But Jesus has power over death and he gave the girl her life back again.

Guess what he told the girl's mother to do? To give her something to eat! After a terrible time in that family everything was back to normal again, and all thanks to the Lord Jesus. (Mark 5:21-43)

- -

BIBLE PROMISE: 'After that, we who are still alive and are left will be caught up together with them in the clouds to meet the Lord in the air. And so we will be with the Lord for ever' (1 Thessalonians 4:17).

45 One day a man was brought to Jesus who was possessed by a demon. That was not uncommon in Jesus' day. The demon prevented the man from being able to speak. Jesus drove the demon out and the man spoke again.

The crowd round about were amazed, but the teachers of the law decided that the demon obeyed Jesus because Jesus was a more powerful demon! Where were their brains? (Matthew 9:32-34)

Demons affected people in all kinds of ways. One sad man spent his life in a graveyard. Find out more about him on the next page.

BIBLE PROMISE: Jesus said, 'If you hold to my teaching, you are really my disciples. Then you will know the truth, and the truth will set you free' (John 8:31-32).

46

This demon-possessed man had amazing strength and he hurt himself in all sorts of ways. Even when people chained him he was able to break free. He cried out in his despair night and day.

When Jesus arrived this poor man fell on the ground in front of him, and yelled at the Lord not to torture him. But as he did so, he called Jesus by name. While men and women don't always recognise who Jesus is, devils do although they don't worship him.

This miracle has a strange ending. The demons were ordered to go into a nearby herd of pigs that then raced down a hillside into the sea and drowned. The people who knew the man saw such an amazing change in him that they were scared of the Lord and asked him to go away! (Mark 5:1-20)

• •

BIBLE PROMISE: 'Therefore, since we have been justified through faith, we have peace with God through our Lord Jesus Christ …' (Romans 5:1).

47 Not all of Jesus' miracles involved making sick people better.

Once a huge crowd followed him to hear his teaching. Over 5,000 men, as well as women and children, were there and they were hungry. Jesus asked his disciples to find out how much food there was in the crowd and they discovered the magnificent total of five bread rolls and two little fish. What could Jesus do with that? He could feed more than 5,000 people, and he did! Not only that, but there were piles of left-overs.

Jesus never does anything by half. (Mark 6:30-44)

BIBLE PROMISE: 'For the LORD is righteous, he loves justice; upright men will see his face' (Psalm 11:7).

48

Once the Lord performed two miracles on the same man at one time. The man was deaf and unable to speak. He had probably been deaf all of his life and so had never been able to learn how to speak. Not only did Jesus give him the gift of hearing, he also gave him the gift of speech. The man was able to say words he had never heard!

That would be like you going to the remotest part of the world and being able to speak to people there, never having heard their language before!

It was also a very kind miracle for it saved people laughing at a grown up trying to learn words for the first time. (Mark 7:31-37)

· ·

BIBLE PROMISE: 'Yet the LORD longs to be gracious to you; he rises to show you compassion. For the LORD is a God of justice. Blessed are all who wait for him!' (Isaiah 30:18).

49 It wasn't unusual to see blind men by the side of the road in Jesus' day, begging for money to buy their food.

Bartimaeus was doing just that at Jericho. He had heard about Jesus and shouted out to the Lord. People told him to be quiet, but the man wouldn't stop shouting. Jesus heard and sent for him. 'What do you want me to do for you?' Jesus asked Bartimaeus. 'I want to see', was his immediate reply.

Jesus knew that the blind man believed in him and he healed him. Imagine this – the first person Bartimaeus saw with his miraculously seeing eyes was the Lord Jesus! I'm sure a look of love passed between them. (Mark 10:46-52)

• •

BIBLE PROMISE: 'O LORD Almighty, blessed is the man who trusts in you' (Psalm 84:12).

50 Jesus had a compassionate heart and we see that in his healing miracles. When he saw a widow woman weeping on her way to bury her only son, he told her not to cry. He then went up to the young man's dead body and ordered him to get up. Life was given back to the woman's son and he sat up and began to talk. (Luke 7:11-17)

Can you just imagine the reaction of the crowd! No wonder news of what happened spread right through the country.

• •

BIBLE PROMISE: God says, 'I am the LORD, and there is no other; apart from me there is no God' (Isaiah 45:5).

51 One Sabbath day, the Lord was in the synagogue and saw a woman who had been bent over for eighteen years. She couldn't straighten up at all. Jesus put his hands on the woman and told her that she was set free from her problem. Immediately she straightened up and praised God. No wonder! (Luke 13:10-17)

Guess what? Some people there were unhappy that Jesus was healing on the Sabbath, even though they would have looked after their farm animals on the Sabbath. People!

• •

BIBLE PROMISE: 'For no matter how many promises God has made, they are "Yes" in Christ' (2 Corinthians 1:20).

52

The Lord Jesus Christ didn't even need to be near people to heal them. He could heal them at a distance.

Once a royal official came to the Lord and asked him to come to his home to heal his dying son. Jesus told the man to go home and that his son would live. Believing what he was told, the official headed for home.

On his way home, some of his servants came to meet him with the news that his son had recovered. And when the official asked for details, he discovered that the boy became better just at the time Jesus said he would. That's amazing! (John 4:43-53)

• •

CHLOE'S QUESTIONS: What was the name of the blind beggar whom Jesus' healed?

BIBLE PROMISE: 'The LORD gives sight to the blind, the LORD lifts up those who are bowed down, the LORD loves the righteous' (Psalm 146:8).

53

You would think that, if a man who was born blind could suddenly see, everyone would be delighted. Not so. The man was. His parents were. But the teachers of the law set up a criminal investigation into the miracle! Eventually the man who had been given the gift of sight became exasperated with them and said about Jesus, 'If this man were not from God, he could do nothing.'

Instead of agreeing with that, the teachers of the law snapped back, 'You were steeped in sin at birth; how dare you lecture us!' Then they threw the man out of the building. Their reaction is almost as amazing as the miracle itself! (John 9:1-41)

CHLOE'S QUESTIONS: Which of the Ten Commandments tells you to rest from your work on the seventh day?

BIBLE PROMISE: 'Give thanks to the LORD, for he is good; his love endures for ever' (Psalm 107:1).

5 4 Jesus had three friends in Bethany, Lazarus and his sisters, Mary and Martha. One day news came to Jesus that Lazarus was sick. By the time he reached Bethany Lazarus was dead and buried. Jesus stood by the tomb and wept.

To everyone's surprise Jesus told the people to take away the stone from the tomb. When that was done, the Lord called to Lazarus to come out. But dead men can't walk! How amazed people must have been when Lazarus obeyed the voice of Jesus and walked out of the tomb, still bound up in his grave clothes. Not even death can stop Jesus. (John 11:1-44)

ABBI'S INFO: In John 12 we read that large crowds came to see Lazarus. And the enemies of Jesus were plotting to kill him as well as Jesus.

BIBLE PROMISE: 'Let us acknowledge the LORD; let us press on to acknowledge him. As surely as the sun rises, he will appear; he will come to us like the winter rains, like the spring rains that water the earth' (Hosea 6:3).

He poured out his life
unto death, and was
numbered with the
transgressors.
(Isaiah 53:12)

THE DEATH OF JESUS

55 Jesus' death was part of the plan of salvation from before the beginning of time. Here are some of the prophecies that were fulfilled at that sad time.

Jesus was betrayed by a friend with whom he had just shared the first Communion bread and wine. (John 13:18). 'Even my close friend, whom I trusted, he who shared my bread, has lifted up his heel against me (Psalm 41:9).

Judas betrayed Jesus for thirty pieces of silver (Matthew 26:14-15). 'I told them, "If you think it best, give me my pay; but if not, keep it." So they paid me thirty pieces of silver' (Zechariah 11:12).

Judas' money went to the potter (Matthew 27:7). 'And the Lord said to me, "Throw it to the potter" – the handsome price at which they priced me! So I took the thirty pieces of silver and threw them into the house of the Lord to the potter' (Zechariah 11:13).

● ●

BIBLE PROMISE: 'I love those who love me, and those who seek me find me' (Proverbs 8:17).

56

Jesus' friends ran away and left him when he needed them most (Matthew 26:56). '"Awake, O sword, against my shepherd, against the man who is close to me!" declares the Lord Almighty. "Strike the shepherd, and the sheep will be scattered ..."' (Zechariah 13:7).

The Lord was accused by false witnesses who told lies to get him into trouble (Matthew 26:59-60). 'O God whom I praise, do not remain silent, for wicked and deceitful men have opened their mouths against me; they have spoken against me with lying tongues' (Psalm 109:1-2).

Jesus was struck on the face by his accusers (Matthew 26:67). 'They will strike Israel's ruler on the cheek with a rod' (Micah 5:1).

For our sakes the Lord was beaten and spat on (Luke 22:63, Matthew 26:67). 'I offered my back to those who beat me, my cheeks to those who pulled out my beard; I did not hide my face from mocking and spitting' (Isaiah 50:6).

• •

BIBLE PROMISE: '... For I will forgive their wickedness and will remember their sins no more' (Jeremiah 31:34).

57

Jesus was silent in the presence of those who accused him (Matthew 27:12-14). 'He was oppressed and afflicted, yet he did not open his mouth; he was led like a lamb to the slaughter, and as a sheep before her shearers is silent, so he did not open his mouth' (Isaiah 53:7).

His hands and feet were pierced as he was nailed to the cross (Luke 23:33). '... a band of evil men has encircled me, they have pierced my hands and my feet' (Psalm 22:16).

• •

ZAC'S CHALLENGE: Look up these verses and copy the words that Jesus said while he was on the cross. Luke 23:34, Luke 23:43, John 19:26-27, Mark 15:34, John 19:28, John 19:30, Luke 23:46.

BIBLE PROMISE: 'The sun will no more be your light by day, nor will the brightness of the moon shine on you, for the LORD will be your everlasting light, and your God will be your glory' (Isaiah 60:19).

5 8 People at the crucifixion said that if Jesus trusted in God, he should ask him to save him (Matthew 27:41-43). 'All who see me ... hurl insults, shaking their heads: "He trusts in the Lord; let the Lord rescue him."' (Psalm 22:7-8).

Jesus prayed for those who were hurting him (Luke 23:34). 'For he bore the sin of many, and made intercession for the transgressors' (Isaiah 53:12). Those who were standing around just shook their heads at him (Matthew 27:39). 'I am an object of scorn to my accusers; when they see me, they shake their heads' (Psalm 109:25).

● ●

CHLOE'S QUESTIONS: Who betrayed Jesus and for how many pieces of silver?

BIBLE PROMISE: Jesus said, '... do not worry about your life, what you will eat or drink; or about your body, what you will wear ... But seek first God's kingdom and his righteousness, and all these things will be given to you as well' (Matthew 6:25, 33).

59 Jesus' clothes were divided between the soldiers by them casting lots (John 19:24). 'They divide my garments among them and cast lots for my clothing' (Psalm 22:18). Casting lots was a way that people made decisions in ancient times. It's similar to flipping a coin.

The Lord Jesus was forsaken by his Father as he bore our sins on the cross (Matthew 27:46). 'My God, my God, why have you forsaken me? Why are you so far from saving me, so far from the words of my groaning?' (Psalm 22:1).

BIBLE PROMISE: Jesus said, 'A new commandment I give you: Love one another. As I have loved you, so you must love one another ... All men will know that you are my disciples if you love one another' (John 13:34-5).

60

It was prophesied that Jesus would be thirsty as he hung on the cross (John 19:28).

'I am worn out calling for help; my throat is parched' (Psalm 69:3).

And hundreds of years before the crucifixion, the psalmist knew that the Lord would be offered gall and vinegar to drink (Matthew 27:34). 'They put gall in my food and gave me vinegar for my thirst' (Psalm 69:21).

BIBLE PROMISE: 'For the wages of sin is death, but the gift of God is eternal life in Christ Jesus our Lord' (Romans 6:23).

61 Jesus' friends were to stand at a distance from the cross (Luke 23:49). 'My friends and companions avoid me because of my wounds; my neighbours stay far away' (Psalm 38:11).

Jesus' side was to be pierced (John 19:34). 'But he was pierced for our transgressions, he was crushed for our iniquities; the punishment that brought us peace was upon him, and by his wounds we are healed' (Isaiah 53:5).

Daylight was to turn to darkness when the Lord was on the cross (Matthew 27:45). '"In that day," declares the Sovereign Lord, "I will make the sun go down at noon and darken the earth in broad daylight"' (Amos 8:9).

And the most amazing fact of all about the crucifixion of the Lord Jesus Christ is that he died on the cross to save his people from their sins. (1 Peter 3:18)

• •

BIBLE PROMISE: Jesus said, 'Blessed are the merciful, for they will be shown mercy' (Matthew 5: 6).

'Let the beloved of the LORD rest secure in him.' (Deuteronomy 33:12)

PRAYER AND PRAYERS

62

Sometimes a whole nation does wrong, perhaps by passing evil laws.

The Hebrew people, whom God had saved from slavery in Egypt, were an ungrateful lot.

The Bible says that they complained about their hardships (this was after they were free!) in the hearing of the Lord God whose righteous anger threatened to destroy them. Moses prayed, asking the Lord not to destroy them, even though they deserved it, and the fire of God died down. (Numbers 11:1-3)

We need to pray about our national sins as well as about our own sins.

• •

BIBLE PROMISE: 'For he will command his angels concerning you to guard you in all your ways ...' (Psalm 91:11).

6 3 Samuel was held in great respect by the Hebrew people and they came to him with their problems.

Once they came demanding that a king be appointed over them. Now, this was something Samuel disapproved of because God was their king. So the wise man went in prayer to the Lord for advice and then followed the advice God gave him.

When we are puzzled we too should go to the Lord for advice, and we'll find it in his Word, the Bible. (1 Samuel 8:1-7)

If you don't yet know your way around the Bible, ask advice from an older Christian who does.

● ●

BIBLE PROMISE: 'Let the beloved of the Lᴏʀᴅ rest secure in him, for he shields him all day long, and the one the Lord loves rests between his shoulders' (Deuteronomy 33:12).

6 4 King Hezekiah also had a problem that he took to the Lord in prayer. Remembering he was speaking to Almighty God, the king began his prayer with worship. Hezekiah's worship prayer is very beautiful. Here's a little part of it. 'O LORD, God of Israel, enthroned between the cherubim, you alone are God over all the kingdoms of the earth. You have made heaven and earth' (2 Kings 19:15).

Only after that did he tell God about his problem.

....

BIBLE PROMISE: God says of those who love him: 'With long life will I satisfy him and show him my salvation' (Psalm 91:16).

6 5 The Book of Psalms is also a book of prayers. In Psalm 23, for example, we overhear King David – who had been a shepherd boy – speaking to the Lord and calling him his shepherd.

David goes on to outline all the ways in which God cares for him. Christians should do that too, look back over their days and thank their Shepherd God for looking after them.

Here's an idea. Every night before you go to bed think of ten things from the day for which you want to thank God.

BIBLE PROMISE: Jesus said, '... the Father himself loves you because you have loved me and have believed that I came from God' (John 16:27).

66 Isaiah had an amazing vision in which he saw something of God's holiness. He realised that in the eyes of such a holy God his heart was very dirty indeed and he cried out in shame.

God sent an angel to purify Isaiah and then an interesting thing happened. The Lord asked for a volunteer! Isaiah, cleansed and ready for service, answered right away. 'Here am I. Send me' (Isaiah 6:8).

God had work for the prophet to do and Isaiah was willing to do it. God has work for every single Christian, and each one of us has to pray Isaiah's prayer, 'Here am I. Send me'.

• •

ABBI'S INFO: God told the disciples to go into the whole world to tell others about Jesus. We must do this too even when people don't want to listen.

BIBLE PROMISE: 'The Lord your God is with you, he is mighty to save. He will take great delight in you, he will quiet you with his love, he will rejoice over you with singing' (Zephaniah 3:17).

67

Jeremiah, who was another of the prophets, believed that God was able to answer his prayer. And there's no point in praying otherwise, is there?

Here's a little of what Jeremiah said. 'Ah, Sovereign Lord, you have made the heavens and the earth by your great power and outstretched arm. Nothing is too hard for you. ... O great and powerful God, whose name is the Lord Almighty, great are your purposes and mighty are your deeds' (Jeremiah 32:17-19).

No problem is too big (or too small) to take to a God as powerful as that!

BIBLE PROMISE: 'Believe in the Lord Jesus, and you will be saved ...' (Acts 16:31).

6 8 When the Lord told Jonah to go somewhere, he headed off in the opposite direction. Then when God insisted, Jonah went into a monumental rage! 'God asked Jonah, "Do you have a right to be angry ... ?" "I do," he said. "I'm angry enough to die."' And that's a splendid example of how not to pray! (Jonah 4:9)

Jesus was very different when he prayed. 'Very early in the morning, while it was still dark, Jesus got up, left the house and went off to a solitary place, where he prayed' (Mark 1:35)

Imagine that! The Lord Jesus, the Son of God, needed to pray! How much more do we?

• •

BIBLE PROMISE: '"Return to me, and I will return to you," says the Lord Almighty' (Malachi 3:7).

69 Jesus told a story about a Pharisee who went to the most public place in the town and made a great show of praying. Jesus said that the only reward he had was that the people thought him very holy. The other man in the story knew he was a sinner and all he did was ask God for mercy. His prayer was heard and answered. (Luke 18:9-14)

. . . .

ABBI'S INFO: In John 17 Jesus prays for his followers, both then and now. 'My prayer is not for them (his disciples) alone. I pray also for those who will believe in me through their message …' Do you realise what that means? The Lord Jesus Christ prays for you and for me! (John 17:20)

BIBLE PROMISE: '… the LORD delights in those who fear him, who put their hope in his unfailing love' (Psalm 147:11). Imagine that! The LORD delights in us!

70

Prayer changes things because God hears and answers. There's a lovely example of that in Acts 10. A man called Cornelius was praying when God spoke to him, telling him to invite Peter to visit. God even gave him Peter's address!

Next day, when Peter was praying, God gave him a vision that the good news about Jesus was to spread beyond the Jewish people to others.

While Peter was puzzling about his vision, Cornelius's messengers arrived inviting him to see their master. Cornelius was not a Jew ... and God had prepared his heart to hear about Jesus at the same time as preparing Peter to tell him!

• •

BIBLE PROMISE: 'Faithfulness springs forth from the earth, and righteousness looks down from heaven. The Lord will indeed give what is good, and our land will yield its harvest' (Psalm 85:11-12).

71

Once, when Peter was in prison, some Christians gathered to pray for his release. Their prayer was answered, Peter was set free, and he went to the house where they were praying. The servant girl dashed into the room to tell them the good news. Their reaction? 'You're out of your mind!' Oops! (Acts 12:1-17)

When we pray we should expect God to answer our prayers.

ABBI'S INFO: Jesus taught his disciples to pray. Read about this in Luke 11:1-4. He taught them what we now call the Lord's Prayer. We don't need to use these exact words every day, but it is a pattern for our prayers.

BIBLE PROMISE: The LORD says, 'I have swept away your offences like a cloud, your sins like the morning mist. Return to me, for I have redeemed you' (Isaiah 44:22).

72

While it's obvious that we should pray for those who are not yet Christians, we discover in the Bible that we should be praying for the church too. If you go to church, you'll know why, because it's made up of ordinary people with all their ups and downs and with all their potential for great things and also great arguments!

Paul prayed that the people in the Colossian church would lead lives worthy of Jesus and please him in every way. (Colossians 1:9-14)

. . . .

ZAC'S CHALLENGE: Start a prayer list or prayer diary where you write down people and places that you want to talk to God about. Remember to thank God for his answers to prayer.

BIBLE PROMISE: God says, 'Can a mother forget the baby at her breast and have no compassion on the child she has borne? Though she may forget, I will not forget you!' (Isaiah 49:15).

God heals the broken-hearted and binds up their wounds. (Psalm 147:3)

MARVELLOUS MOUNTAINS

73 Noah and his family built a huge boat that was used to rescue his family along with two of each of God's creatures. After forty days and nights of rain it took a very long time for the waters to begin to go down.

Months of drying wind later, the boat – it was called Noah's ark – bumped on to dry land on the mountains of Ararat. It took another three months before the water subsided enough for the eight people on board the ark to see the top of the mountain on which they had landed! (Genesis 8:1-5)

• •

BIBLE PROMISE: 'For men are not cast off by the Lord for ever. Though he brings grief, he will show compassion, so great is his unfailing love. For he does not willingly bring affliction or grief to the children of men' (Lamentations 3:31-33).

74

By the time his son Isaac was born Abraham was old enough to be his great, great, great, great grandfather! When Isaac was still quite young, God told Abraham to do a very strange thing. He told him to take Isaac to a mountain and sacrifice him as an offering there. But the Lord didn't want Isaac sacrificed, he wanted Abraham's faith tested. Abraham passed the test.

As Abraham raised his knife, the Lord called from heaven and told him not to lay a hand on the boy. A ram caught in a nearby bush was used as the offering instead. God provided the ram. (Genesis 22:1-18).

BIBLE PROMISE: God says, 'I will make an everlasting covenant with them: I will never stop doing good to them, and I will inspire them to fear me, so that they will never turn away from me. I will rejoice in doing them good ...' (Jeremiah 32:40-41).

75

When God wanted to do something special he often chose a hill or a mountain on which to do it.

On one occasion the Amalekites attacked God's people. As the battle raged, Moses stood on top of a hill at Rephidim holding his stick in the air. As long as he held it up the Israelites were winning, but as soon as he rested his arms the Amalekites overpowered them. The day went on and Moses grew so tired he was given a stone to sit on.

Later, as he grew even more tired, two of the Israelite leaders stood, one on either side of Moses, holding his hands up. On top of the mountain at Rephidim Moses held his stick in the air until evening and the battle was won. (Exodus 17:8-16)

● ●

ABBI'S INFO: Moses was at least eighty years old when he led the Israelites out of Egypt.

BIBLE PROMISE: God 'heals the broken-hearted and binds up their wounds' (Psalm 147:3).

76

Three months after Pharaoh let God's people leave Egypt Moses, their leader, climbed Mount Sinai and the Lord spoke to him there. God gave Moses the Ten Commandments. While they spoke Mount Sinai was covered with smoke. There was thunder and lightning and the whole mountain shook. (Exodus 19-20)

Why did the mountain shake? Perhaps it was so excited that the Lord God, who made it, was there.

BIBLE PROMISE: Jesus said, 'Peace I leave with you; my peace I give you. I do not give to you as the world gives. Do not let your hearts be troubled and do not be afraid' (John 14:27).

77 Just before the people went into the Promised Land Moses, who was by then an old man, climbed Mount Nebo. From there he could see the land the Lord was giving to his people.

Although Moses saw the Promised Land he never entered it, for he died before the people crossed the River Jordan into their new homeland. Moses was taken to a far better place. He was taken home to heaven to be with the Lord forever. (Deuteronomy 34:1-5)

• •

ABBI'S INFO: Look up Matthew 3:13-17 and find out who was baptized in the River Jordan.

BIBLE PROMISE: 'Since, then, you have been raised with Christ, set your hearts on things above, where Christ is seated at the right hand of God. Set your minds on things above, not on earthly things. For you died, and your life is now hidden with Christ in God. When Christ, who is your life, appears, then you also will appear with him in glory' (Colossians 3:1-4).

78 Imagine two hills with a valley in between and with the Philistine army camped on top of one hill and the Israelite army on top of the other.

Every day Goliath, the Philistine champion, went down into the valley and made fun of the Israelites because none of them were brave enough to fight him. And no wonder, for he was a very big strong man!

David, who was possibly just a teenager visiting his soldier brothers, trusted God to help him. With only a slingshot and stones he killed Goliath and the Philistine army turned and ran away! (1 Samuel 17)

BIBLE PROMISE: 'Love the LORD, all his saints! The LORD preserves the faithful, but the proud he pays back in full. Be strong and take heart, all you who hope in the LORD' (Psalm 31:23-24).

79 The prophet Elijah and the false prophets of the idol Baal prepared bulls for burnt offerings to be sacrificed, but Elijah soaked his with water! That certainly wouldn't help it to burn. However, after the prophets of Baal had failed to get their 'god' to burn up their sacrifice it was Elijah's turn. He prayed to the one true God and the Lord sent fire down from heaven that set the soaking sacrifice ablaze! (1 Kings 18:16-46)

Elijah saw God winning a mighty victory on Mount Carmel.

• •

CHLOE'S QUESTIONS: On what mountain did God give Moses the Ten Commandments?

BIBLE PROMISE: The Lord says, 'Before they call I will answer; while they are still speaking I will hear' (Isaiah 65:24).

80

Jerusalem, the city of David, was built on Mount Zion. Cities built on mountains were safer than those built on flat land as enemy armies could be seen in the distance.

Jerusalem, perched on Mount Zion, was besieged more than once and was able to hold out for a very long time.

Yet, when King David thought back, he knew that it was God who had been his refuge, not hills or caves, and that even if the mountains were to fall into the heart of the sea God would still care for him. (Psalm 46:1-3)

• •

ABBI'S INFO: Mount Moriah appears in another famous Bible story. Read Genesis chapter 22 to find out about it.

BIBLE PROMISE: 'For sin shall not be your master, because you are not under law, but under grace' (Romans 6:14).

81 King Nebuchadnezzar of Babylon had a dream that troubled him. Not only did he want his wise men to tell him what the dream meant, but he wanted them to tell him what the dream was! Of course, none of them could do that ... apart from Daniel, to whom God showed the King's dream.

King Nebuchadnezzar had dreamed of a huge statue that was broken down by a rock that became as big as a mountain.

Daniel told the king that his dream was to show him that although Nebuchadnezzar's kingdom was huge like that statue, the kingdom God would set up would crush all other kingdoms and bring them to an end. (Daniel 2:24-45)

BIBLE PROMISE: 'Do not grieve, for the joy of the LORD is your strength' (Nehemiah 8:10).

82

Large crowds of people followed the Lord Jesus when he began to teach and preach and heal people with all kinds of diseases.

Once there was such a crowd that Jesus went up on a mountain, sat down, and taught the people.

Matthew wrote down much of what Jesus said that day and it takes up a whole three chapters of his gospel. It is called the Sermon on the Mount. Because the Lord was on a mountainside the great crowd would be able to see him and hear what he was saying. (Matthew 5–7)

ABBI'S INFO: You can pray to God anywhere but Jesus gives some good advice about where you should pray. Read Matthew 6:6.

BIBLE PROMISE: 'The ransomed of the Lord will return. They will enter Zion with singing; everlasting joy will crown their heads. Gladness and joy will overtake them, and sorrow and sighing will flee away' (Isaiah 51:11).

8 3 Jesus told a story about a shepherd who had a hundred sheep. Ninety-nine were safe in the sheepfold, but one was lost. The shepherd went out into the hills, searched until he found the lost sheep and brought it safely home. (Matthew 18:10-14)

The Lord Jesus, who is the Good Shepherd, came down from heaven to die on the cross in order that he could take every one of his sheep home to heaven one day.

BIBLE PROMISE: '... I know whom I have believed, and am convinced that he is able to guard what I have entrusted to him for that day' (2 Timothy 1:12).

84 A few weeks after the Lord Jesus rose from the dead, he met with his disciples on the Mount of Olives. Before their eyes they saw Jesus being taken up to heaven. They watched amazed until a cloud hid him from their sight. They were still staring up into the sky when two men in white appeared beside them and told them that, just as they had seen Jesus go to heaven, one day he would return.

Christians are still waiting for, and longing for, the great day when the Lord Jesus will return in glory. (Acts 1:9-11)

• •

BIBLE PROMISE: 'Yet I am always with you; you hold me by my right hand. You guide me with your counsel, and afterwards you will take me into glory' (Psalm 73:23-24).

'I am the
resurrection
and the life.'
(John 11:25)

CREATURES GREAT AND SMALL

85 Think of all the animals you can – from tall giraffes to tiny mice, from huge elephants to slim-line snakes, from monkeys with one pair of arms and legs to centipedes, from dogs that bark to bulls that bellow … and the first of all their kinds was made in just ONE day by the Lord our God! All animals that live on the earth, mankind included, were made on the sixth day of creation. (Genesis 1:24-27)

After God made Adam the Lord brought all the creatures he had made to him to be named. Naming the animals and birds was one of the first jobs the very first man had to do. What a lot of names he had to think up! (Genesis 2:19-20)

• •

BIBLE PROMISE: Jesus said, 'I am the resurrection and the life. He who believes in me will live, even though he dies; and whoever lives and believes in me, will never die' (John 11:25-26).

86

Did you know that a serpent (snake) used to have legs? Satan came in the form of a serpent to tempt Eve in the Garden of Eden. God had told Adam that they should not eat of the Tree of the Knowledge of Good and Evil because, if they did, they would die.

Satan persuaded Eve that God had not said that at all, and she ate the forbidden fruit. God cursed Satan for the terrible thing he had done. Part of the curse was, 'You will crawl on your belly ... all the days of your life' (Genesis 3:14).

If the serpent only started crawling on his belly after he was cursed, he must have had legs before that!

BIBLE PROMISE: 'For Christ died for sins once for all, the righteous for the unrighteous, to bring you to God' (1 Peter 3:18).

87 When Noah completed the ark according to the building instructions God had given him, the Lord told him to take seven of every clean animal and two of every unclean animal into the ark, as well as seven of every kind of bird.

He had to take males and females (of course!) in order that after the flood God's creatures would be able to breed and restock the earth. (Genesis 7:2-3)

All the animals that live on the earth today are descended from those Noah took into the ark with him.

BIBLE PROMISE: Jesus said, 'And surely I will be with you always, to the very end of the age' (Matthew 28:20).

88 God can use animals in answer to prayer. When Abraham was old he wanted to find a good wife for his son Isaac. Abraham asked his trusted servant to go a very long journey back to his homeland to find a suitable girl.

The servant, who trusted in the Lord, prayed a really strange prayer as he approached a spring of water. He prayed that the right girl would give him a drink of water from the spring and offer to water his camels too. She did, and her name was Rebekah.

Rebekah went back home with Abraham's servant and married Isaac. (Genesis 24:12-14)

· ·

BIBLE PROMISE: God says, 'Those who honour me I will honour, but those who despise me will be disdained' (1 Samuel 2:30).

89 Pharaoh would not set the Israelite slaves free. He was hard-hearted and God hardened his heart even more. The Lord sent a plague on Egypt every time Pharaoh refused to let God's people go.

The second plague was a plague of frogs. They were everywhere! There were frogs in streets and in houses, in beds and in ovens. Frogs even managed to jump into the dishes where bread dough was being mixed!

Pharaoh didn't like the frogs one little bit and he told Moses to pray the frogs away and then he would let the people go. Moses prayed and the Lord took away the frogs but Pharaoh did not let the Israelite people go. (Exodus 8:1-15)

BIBLE PROMISE: 'My son, do not forget my teaching, but keep my commands in your heart, for they will prolong your life many years and bring you prosperity' (Proverbs 3:1-2).

90

The plagues sent by the Lord seemed to harden Pharaoh's heart even more. But each plague brought with it a very special miracle.

The Hebrew slaves, God's chosen people, lived in Egypt along with the Egyptians. Yet when the Lord sent his plagues they only affected Pharaoh and the people of Egypt, never God's people or their animals.

One of the plagues killed all the livestock that belonged to the Egyptians, but the animals that belonged to the Israelites were absolutely fine! (Exodus 9:1-6)

• •

BIBLE PROMISE: The LORD says, 'Even to your old age and grey hairs I am he, I am he who will sustain you. I have made you and I will carry you; I will sustain you and I will rescue you' (Isaiah 46:4).

91

Each plague was worse than the one that had gone before, and there were ten altogether. The tenth plague was truly awful.

God said that, if Pharaoh didn't let the Israelite people go, the oldest child in every Egyptian family, both human and animal, would die.

God had a very different plan for his own special people. He gave instructions for each family to kill a lamb, and to mark the door of their house with the lamb's blood, before roasting it for a very important feast. The feast was called the Passover, because that night the Angel of Death passed over the houses of the Israelites.

After that terrible night Pharaoh did let God's people go. (Exodus 12:1-30)

• •

CHLOE'S QUESTIONS: What was the second plague?

BIBLE PROMISE: '... who forgives all your sins and heals all your diseases; who redeems your life from the pit and crowns you with love and compassion' (Psalm 103:3-4).

92

Every single man and woman, boy and girl, is a sinner and all deserve to be punished by being banished from the Lord our God for time and for eternity. That's a terrible thing.

The Bible tells us an amazing fact. Jesus becomes the Passover lamb for each and every person who confesses his or her sins and trusts in the Lord as Saviour! And because Jesus is the Christian's Passover lamb, the believer's punishment is passed over. He goes straight to heaven when he dies and remains there in the joy and glory of Jesus for ever and ever and ever. (1 Corinthians 5:7)

• •

ZAC'S CHALLENGE: Draw a picture of a Bible Zoo – here are a few animals to get you started. Look up these Bible verses: Proverbs 6;6, 1 Samuel 17:34-36, 1 Peter 5:8, Matthew 7:15. Add some other animals too.

BIBLE PROMISE: 'In your unfailing love you will lead the people you have redeemed. In your strength you will guide them to your holy dwelling' (Exodus 15:13).

93

Did you know that one of God's Ten Commandments has to do with an ox and a donkey? It's a fact!

The tenth Commandment tells us that we mustn't always be wishing for what other people have. Imagine you were living back in the time of Moses and that you were not very well off. You might look at your rich neighbour and wish that you owned the strong servant who did his work, or the ox that pulled his plough or the donkey that carried his bags. (Exodus 20:17)

God commands us not to long for what other people have, but rather to be content with what he has given us.

• •

ZAC'S CHALLENGE: Look up these Bible passages to find examples of coveting (wanting) what belongs to someone else leading to serious sins. Joshua 7 and 2 Samuel 11.

BIBLE PROMISE: Jesus told Thomas, who had not at first believed the Lord had been raised from the dead, 'Because you have seen me, you have believed; blessed are those who have not seen and yet have believed' (John 20:29).

94 Have you ever thought that evil idols are made from God's creation? They all are, because God created absolutely everything.

Not very long after the wonderful time when Mount Sinai shook and God gave Moses the Ten Commandments for his people, Moses was again up the mountain with the Lord. He was away for so long that the people asked Aaron (Moses' brother) to make 'gods' – idols! – for them to worship. Imagine that!

They gave Aaron their gold jewellery and he melted it down and then made it into the shape of a calf and they worshipped it. What a dreadful thing to do! The people took the gold that God had created and made an idol in the shape of a calf God had created. (Exodus 32:1-8)

How angry the Lord must have been, and how careful we should be not to turn God's good gifts into idols that we love more than we love him.

• •

BIBLE PROMISE: 'But the Lord is faithful, and he will strengthen and protect you from the evil one' (2 Thessalonians 3:3).

9 5 Until the coming of the Lord Jesus Christ as a baby at Bethlehem, those who wanted to ask God to forgive their sins did so by offering an animal sacrifice. Before they sacrificed the animal, they laid their hand on its head as though passing their sin on to the animal.

These animal sacrifices were pictures of what was to come when, on the cross, the Lord Jesus took the sins of all who will believe on him. It is only through his death on the cross that his people's sins are taken away, and they are taken away for ever. (Leviticus 1)

· ·

ABBI'S INFO: Because some people in Bible times were too poor to give the offering of a lamb, God allowed them to offer turtledoves or pigeons instead (Leviticus 5:7). We know that Mary and Joseph were not rich because that was the sacrifice they offered when Jesus was presented at the temple (Luke 2:22-24).

BIBLE PROMISE: 'For the LORD is righteous, he loves justice; upright men will see his face' (Psalm 11:7).

117

96

Once the children of Israel were being particularly rebellious. In order to teach them a lesson God sent poisonous snakes among them. The people realised the snakes had been sent as a punishment and were really sorry for what they had said and done.

When Moses prayed for them God told him to make a bronze snake and put it on a pole, and that anyone who looked on the snake would not die from the effects of snake venom.

Moses did what he was told and made a bronze snake which he attached to a pole. After that, anyone who was bitten by a snake looked at the bronze snake and lived. (Numbers 21:4-9)

BIBLE PROMISE: 'As a father has compassion on his children, so the LORD has compassion on those who fear him; for he knows how we are formed, he remembers that we are dust' (Psalm 103:13-14).

97 Did you know that a talking donkey once saw an angel? It's a fact!

Once a man called Balaam was going, by donkey, where God didn't want him to go. God sent an angel to stop him. His donkey saw the angel and turned off the road into a field. Balaam was cross and beat her.

Then, as they went along a narrow road with walls on both sides, the angel appeared again. The donkey crushed Balaam's foot against the wall as her rider tried to make her go past the angel and he beat her once again.

Next the angel stood in the narrowest bit of the road and Balaam's donkey could not get past. She lay down in front of the angel – and was beaten once again.

The donkey turned round and asked her master why she had been beaten three times! What a shock Balaam must have had. But it was only when God opened Balaam's eyes to see the angel for himself that he understood why the donkey had behaved the way she had. (Numbers 22:21-41)

• •

BIBLE PROMISE: God says, 'Do not be afraid, for I am with you …' (Isaiah 43:5).

98 The puzzle of the live bees and the dead lion. Strong Samson was one of God's mighty judges. When Samson was on his way to be married he passed a dead lion. Now, he had been told by the Lord never to touch any dead animals. But his curiosity got the better of him and he went to look at the lion. When he got there he discovered a swarm of bees in the carcass and he ate some of their honey. Not only did he touch a dead animal, but he ate something from inside it! That was a really stupid thing to do.

At the wedding Samson made up a riddle for the young men who were there, and here it is. 'Out of the eater, something to eat; out of the strong, something sweet.' The young men couldn't answer the riddle – but you can. Out of the eater (the lion that eats other creatures) something to eat (honey); out of the strong (the lion is a very strong animal), something sweet (that honey again). Perhaps you didn't know that there was a riddle in the Bible. (Judges 14:8-20)

● ●

BIBLE PROMISE: Jesus says, 'In the same way, I tell you, there is rejoicing in the presence of the angels of God over one sinner who repents' (Luke 15:10).

99 David was still a young man when he killed Goliath, but that was not the first brave thing he had done. 'When a lion or a bear came and carried off a sheep from the flock, I went after it, struck it and rescued the sheep from its mouth. When it turned on me, I seized it by its hair, struck it and killed it.'

David knew where his power came from, 'The Lord who delivered me from the paw of the lion and the paw of the bear will deliver me from the hand of this Philistine' (Goliath). And he did! (1 Samuel 17:34-36, 37)

BIBLE PROMISE: '... everyone who believes in him (Jesus) may have eternal life' (John 3:15).

100

Nehemiah was sent by the Lord to organise the rebuilding of the broken walls of the city of Jerusalem. As the people worked they had to endure the nasty teasing of several unpleasant men who tried to interrupt what they were doing. One of them, he was called Tobiah, sneered at the newly built wall. 'If even a fox climbed up on it, he would break down their wall of stones!' Not a nice man, Tobiah. (Nehemiah 4:3)

Perhaps you are teased because you go to church or Sunday School, or because you come from a Christian home or read your Bible. Don't let unchristian people stop you from doing what God wants you to do. Insults are not nice, but they are only words. And that's a fact!

BIBLE PROMISE: 'For this is what the Sovereign Lord says: "I myself will search for my sheep and look after them. As a shepherd looks after his scattered flock when he is with them, so will I look after my sheep"' (Ezekiel 34:11-12).

101

The book of Job in the Bible is the story of a man to whom terrible things happened. Poor Job was in a bad way, made even worse by his three 'friends' who came to help and comfort him. Unfortunately they knew exactly the wrong things to say and were no comfort at all.

Eventually God spoke directly to Job, reminding him that it is the Lord who provides food for the ravens, who watches the deer as her fawn is born, who made the great wings of the ostrich, who gave the horse its strength and the locust its ability to leap so high. (Job 39)

Because of all his problems Job was looking in at himself rather than God. By pointing his servant to the wonders of his creation, the Lord pointed him back to the One who made him.

When you feel that life is getting on top of you, look around at God's wonderful world and remember that the One who made it is more wonderful still.

• •

BIBLE PROMISE: 'The LORD gives strength to his people; the LORD blessed his people with peace' (Psalm 29:11).

102

The story of Jonah contains an amazing fact – that Jonah stayed alive inside a big fish for three days until the fish vomited him up on the shore. How did he get there?

God told Jonah to go to Nineveh with a message for the people there but Jonah headed off, by ship, in the opposite direction. The Lord sent a storm that filled the ship's sailors with fear. Jonah admitted that it was his fault for disobeying the Lord, and agreed to be thrown overboard into the sea.

The big fish was sent to save Jonah's life ... and then he went where God told him to go. It would have been so much easier for him had Jonah done what the Lord wanted him to do first time round! (Jonah 1:15—2:10)

BIBLE PROMISE: A promise about heaven – 'He will wipe every tear from their eyes. There will be no more death or mourning or crying or pain, for the old order of things has passed away' (Revelation 21:4).

103

One day some people were discussing whether or not the Lord Jesus should pay tax to the government, and Jesus joined in the discussion. He was due to pay two drachma in tax.

Jesus told Peter to go down to the lake and catch a fish. Peter must have been very surprised to be told that he would find a four drachma coin in the fish's mouth and that he had to pay Jesus' tax and his own tax with it.

Guess what? There was a coin in the mouth of the very first fish he caught! (Matthew 17:24-27)

• •

ZAC'S CHALLENGE: Write the words of Isaiah 53:6. Cut up the sheet of paper, jumble the pieces and then put the jigsaw together. Time yourself each time you do it.

BIBLE PROMISE: '"You will seek me and find me when you seek me with all your heart. I will be found by you," declares the LORD, "and will bring you back from captivity"' (Jeremiah 29:13-14).

104

Jesus told a story one day in order to teach a fascinating fact. He said that when the Son of Man (that's the Lord himself) comes back in glory there will be a great day of judgment in which people will be divided into two groups, just as a shepherd separates his sheep from his goats.

The sheep will be taken home to heaven and the goats will not. The sheep are God's people who trust in him and live their lives for him. (Matthew 25:31-46)

That story should make us ask ourselves a really important question. Have we asked Jesus to forgive our sins and be our Saviour? If not, today is the best day to do that.

. . . .

BIBLE PROMISE: 'For the LORD is good and his love endures for ever; his faithfulness continues through all generations' (Psalm 100:5).

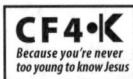